We Used to Be Generals

we used to be generals

Sarah Campbell

To "my friends pictured within," met and unmet

(from Elgar's dedication of the Enigma Variations*)*

WHAT HAPPENS WHEN NOTHING HAPPENS

This is where I was
The soil falling off of my head

FRAMED AND GLAZED

Spell, fall, sling
Fool

Compose yourself
Life is like this

WE USED TO BE GENERALS

Sifting through minerals and gems
More before meant less thereafter

When then they were there
And then there were none

1 IN 8 MILLION

Tears in the clouds
A moving cathedral of chairs

Ladies and gentlemen
We are the traffic

FORKING IT OVER

Today this was true
That is that

Gave them yesterday too

MIGHT AS WELL

Sings the matter
To the will

OPEN LETTER UNDER GROUND

Are you on your way?
Protect yourself
Don't keep it to yourself

MARK THESE WORDS

'If'
'Only'
'Once'
Then get lost

FROM THE BEGINNING

Not anybody
A body
Halves the difference
Believes the world contains at least three things

SUNDAY

The oldest trick in the book

THE GREATEST OF ALL GREAT

We saw our plans
Where they would have been
Had we not been still living

EATING THE COMPANY'S CAKE

Back to back
They call me theirs
Up to my neck in shoulders

WHEN WE WERE CHILDREN

Enough was never enough
Hours, barbaric and blooming
The hole of it
All that waiting around

SHE LEFT, SHE ARRIVED

No matter
Fatter
Outriding out there
Beyond the thirty valley

THE UNMET FRIEND

All alone
Like a small incendiary device

THE TRAMPOLINE IN HIM

Five horns
Six when he wasn't singing

DOING THINGS THAT MAKE US MORE LIKE OURSELVES

Don't forget to write something I won't

ONE UNFIELDED BALE

We made it ring
Gave it a shot
Stood it up
Floored it

WAIT FOR ME

Caught in the fact
Passed out on the lawn
Of what I wanted to say

WE WERE DIFFERENT ENOUGH WITHOUT THE DIFFERENCES

I—
Here it's beautiful
Where you are

THE PRINCE HE WAS

Among even the flattening crowd
But no one was interested in classes
Or complexes

IS THE WORLD OVER?

Left with the lights on

When love is an obstacle
We'll pretend we never knew

THE CONSOLATIONS OF ADVENTURE STORIES

What can I say
I say
I have enjoyed every minute so far

TELL ME WHERE THE LIE IS

Between
What can be said
Dragon fly
What can be shown
Flown

THE LAST OF THE REST OF THE EARTH

Or so they saw
Unbolted and out of hand
Dragging the meteorite home in ropes

CORRECTION

You are not my consolation
Other people's lives look better than
Other people's lives
The mind is an argument all its own

FOX

Falcon

SAILOR SOLDIER

Sockless albatross
Hauling wings at your side
We don't understand

BEFORE THE LAST SUPPER

Warbler
Going gone
When you know it and you're happy
Clap your hands

RECOLLECTIONS OF A GEOGRAPHER

That you stood back to see if I would
Under all those flares
Knocking down cairns

SHOW OVER

Palms aweigh
Feet in the air
That's how you do
"How do you do"

THE WOLF IN MY HEAD

Four hundred miles strong
All in a ditch

EACH SENTENCE THINKS

A failure of imagination
Falling out with itself

WHY I NEEDED AN ENEMY

Talk to me

THE PEOPLE HELD THEIR PLANET HEADS UP

In our anger
We hoped
We were against hope

THE DAY I DECIDED TO STOP LOOKING AT ALL OF YOU

Out the window
Saw it coming

THE APPEARANCE OF APPEARANCE

Niagara Falls for one
Imagine that

YOU'RE BREAKING UP

I love you anyway
Your flag hand waving
The end like a flag

THERE THEY GO

Not turning out
Not trying
And a whole church involved

IF DEMENTIA WERE A COUNTRY

When are becomes is
Let me introduce myself

AS SEEN WATCHING TV

And nothing at all will happen again
Then

WHAT ISN'T ANYMORE

Alights

Giraffes we didn't learn to ride
The French we took
The done-and-gone fastnesses of the forest

HERE'S TO SOMETIME

Drop your stilts
Say yes

THIS IS WHAT YOU WILL DO

Second thought not best
First thought was
That I am

ADVICE TO THE ONE WHO GOT HER CROWN BACK

Like a grave in the ground
Cover it

Further Other Book Works
200 W 55th 1/2 St.
Austin, TX 78751
http://www.furtherotherbookworks.tumblr.com

First printing April 2014
ISBN-13: 978-0-9893132-1-6
Library of Congress Control Number: 2014930279

Acknowledgments:
A few of these poems were published at joylandpoetry.com.

Also by Sarah Campbell:
Everything We Could Ask For (2010)
The Maximum (2008)